PORTRAIT OF
SHREWSBURY

ROBIN JUKES-HUGHES MBE
STAN SEDMAN MBE

HALSGROVE

First published in Great Britain in 2013

Copyright © Robin Jukes-Hughes and Stan Sedman 2013

British Library Cataloguing-in-Publication Data
A CIP record for this title is available from the British Library

ISBN 978 0 85704 205 7

HALSGROVE
Halsgrove House,
Ryelands Business Park,
Bagley Road, Wellington, Somerset TA21 9PZ
Tel: 01823 653777   Fax: 01823 216796
email: sales@halsgrove.com

Part of the Halsgrove group of companies
Information on all Halsgrove titles is available at: www.halsgrove.com

Printed and bound in China by Everbest Printing Co Ltd

INTRODUCTION

SHREWSBURY – HISTORIC COUNTY TOWN OF SHROPSHIRE

Shrewsbury is the County Town of Shropshire and one of England's finest medieval and Tudor towns. It has the great advantage of being almost completely surrounded by the River Severn, and this has protected the town throughout the ages from assault and from undue development. As a result Shrewsbury has retained much of its charm and many of its old buildings. There are no fewer than 660 listed buildings within the loop of the river – one of the highest concentrations in the country.

The town was first recorded in writing as Civitate Scrobbensis in 901, although it was certainly inhabited well before this. After the Norman Conquest William the Conqueror presented the town to his kinsman Roger de Montgomery, making him Earl of Shrewsbury, the premier earldom of England. Montgomery built a massive castle to guard the two fords over the river and turned the town into a fortress from which to control the Welsh border. It became one of the three main Marcher Castles, together with Chester and Hereford, and was engaged in constant warfare over the next two centuries.

Shrewsbury prospered during the medieval period and by the end of the fourteenth century it had become one of the twelve wealthiest towns in England. It continued to be an important base for English forces engaged in wars against the Welsh, and the castle and town walls were both heavily fortified during this period. The Battle of Shrewsbury in 1403, made famous by William Shakespeare in *Henry IV* Part 1, was one of the bloodiest battles in English history.

The Tudors ushered in a more peaceful period, and the town prospered greatly from cornering a lucrative trade in Welsh wool. Many wool merchants, drapers, and clothiers became very rich during the period and built fine mansions and public buildings. The town fell to Parliamentarian forces in 1645 during the Civil War, and soon afterwards the wool trade went into decline.

Shrewsbury prospered again after the Restoration when it became the centre of a thriving coach trade between London and Holyhead and a fashionable resort for the gentry. Many of their fine Georgian and Queen Anne mansions are still in use today as private residences. The town's most famous son, the scientist Charles Darwin, was born at the Mount in 1809 and was a pupil at Shrewsbury School.

The railways came to Shrewsbury in 1848 and established it as a major rail centre for the West Coast and Wales, which brought increased prosperity to the area. Shrewsbury today is a thriving market town and the focus of commercial and agricultural activity for the surrounding area and much of Mid Wales. Recent years have seen a big expansion in the retail trade and tourism, and since World War II it has become famous internationally as a Town of Flowers.

This book begins with a journey down the picturesque River Severn. It goes on to look at some of the peerless buildings from the medieval, Tudor, Georgian, Victorian and modern periods before focussing on its internationally-famous role as "The Town of Flowers". It concludes with a look at some of the major attractions around the town, and the beautiful setting that has done so much to influence the development of this most quintessentially English town.

Robin Jukes-Hughes
Stan Sedman, 2013

SHREWSBURY

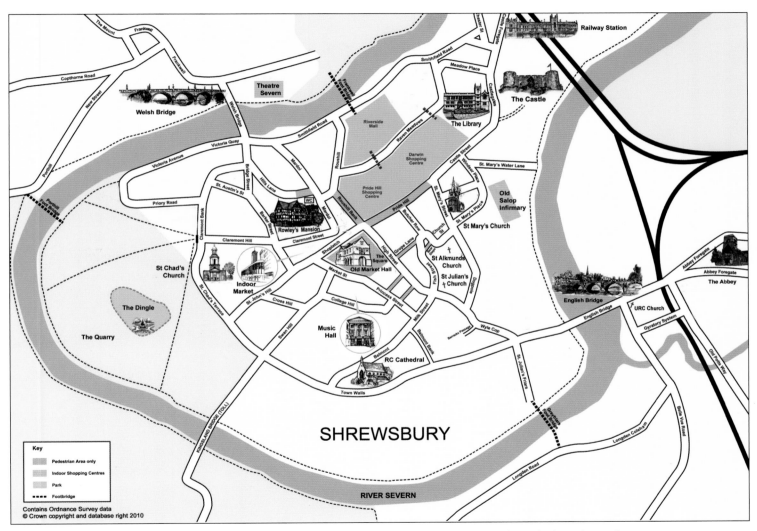

The street pattern within the loop of the River Severn was substantially built up before the Reformation.
Apart from street-widening and minor alterations, there has been very little change since. Many of the
medieval street names, such as Dogpole, Mardol, Shoplatch and Wyle Cop, are still in use today.

Shrewsbury and the River Severn from Coton Hill

THE RIVER SEVERN

Shrewsbury owes its existence to the River Severn. The wide river almost completely surrounds the town, leaving a landward approach only 300 yards wide which can easily be commanded by a castle on the hill overlooking it. In early days the river protected the town from attack, and in more peaceful times it became an important means of travel and communications, especially for the wool trade. River traffic went into decline as other forms of transport developed, and the river is now used mainly for sport and leisure activities.

This scene of the River Severn and its water meadows, with Shrewsbury Castle on the left of the image and the twin spires of St Mary's and St Alkmund's on the skyline, has changed little since medieval times.

The Welsh Bridge from Frankwell Footbridge

This five-arch stone bridge was built by local stonemasons Carline and Tilley in 1792-95. It replaced the massive and heavily fortified medieval St George's Bridge which crossed the river at the bottom of the Mardol. The medieval bridge was made famous by J.M.W. Turner in his painting *The Old Welsh Bridge* of 1794, in which the present bridge can be seen under construction through the arches of the old.

The Welsh Bridge at Sunset

The new Welsh Bridge was constructed downstream from St George's Bridge against the advice of the famous civil engineer, Thomas Telford. Its foundations were laid on oak platforms 12 inches thick sitting on the river bed, on what civil engineers call 'raft foundations'. By 1831 the bed of the river under the central arch was in danger of being washed away by the force of the river in flood. The bridge was saved from imminent destruction by depositing barge loads of huge rocks around the foundations.

Quantum Leap

This iconic sculpture was built to commemorate the bicentenary of Darwin's birth at the Mount in Shrewsbury on 12 February 1809. The ribs were cast from ground granite and concrete, which were then sandblasted and mounted on a steel core. The design is open to interpretation and can be likened to a human vertebra, dinosaur's skeleton, DNA or a shell. It is located in a new 'geo-garden', celebrating Shropshire's long geological history in which ten of the thirteen internationally recognised geological periods are represented.

The New Theatre Severn

Theatre Severn opened in March 2009 on Frankwell Quay, a stunning riverside location alongside one of the main gateways into the town. It is built on the site of the old St George's Bridge, and part of the medieval bridge survives under the stage area. The theatre has a main auditorium, a smaller theatre used for talks and audio visual shows, a state-of-the-art dance studio and an exhibition gallery. It is well appointed with bars and restaurants and is proving very popular.

Victoria Quay from the Welsh Bridge

Victoria Avenue was created in 1904 through what were once the Priory Gardens alongside the river, and it is now one of the main entrances into the Quarry Park. The landing stage for the river cruise launch *Sabrina* was constructed more recently. The Armoury Restaurant, which can be seen beyond *Sabrina*, began life in 1806 as an armoury on the outskirts of the town for the purpose of housing the weapons of local militia. There was a shortage of building bricks at the end of the First World War, so Morris & Co bought the building and dismantled it prior to rebuilding it on its current site.

The Boathouse Inn
This Grade II listed building dates from the late sixteenth century and is recorded as being used as a 'pest house' in 1650 to isolate victims of the Great Plague. It was popular with barge traffic along the river for many years and became a public house in the eighteenth century. A ferry operated from the lawn for two hundred years prior to the construction of Porthill Footbridge in 1923 to take passengers to the town.

Porthill Footbridge
This is a traditional suspension bridge with steel cables suspended between two towers, 10 feet apart,
and measures 200 feet between the towers. The rigidity of its deck is provided by the lattice girder parapets.
It was opened on 18 January 1923 at a cost of £2,600.

The Welsh Bridge from Porthill Footbridge
A late evening image of the Welsh Bridge and Theatre Severn taken from Porthill Footbridge.

Victoria Avenue

The original walks were created in 1719 with lime trees planted on both sides to give shade from the sun. Further walks and trees were added subsequently. Shortly after Percy Thrower arrived as Town Parks Superintendent in 1946 he found that the original lime trees were unsafe and had them felled and replaced with new limes at 20 foot instead of 10 foot intervals.

Pengwern Boathouse
This boathouse was built by Pengwern Rowing Club in 1881. The Shrewsbury Rowing Regatta has taken place here annually since 1889, and attracts competitors from all over the country.

Shrewsbury School and Boathouse

The main building of Shrewsbury School was built by Thomas Farnolls Pritchard 1760-5 as a Foundling Hospital for London orphans to be trained to work in the wool trade. It closed in 1772 when it ran out of money, and was purchased by the town in 1784 and converted to a House of Industry (a workhouse for the poor). Shrewsbury School, which was housed in cramped conditions in the centre of town, purchased the building and moved there in 1882. The boathouse was bought from Pengwern Rowing Club and extended in memory of Lt Pugh, an ex-student, who was killed in 1918 aged nineteen years.

Kingsland Toll Bridge

This privately owned toll bridge was built by Cleveland Bridge & Engineering Company (who built Sydney Harbour and Victoria Falls bridges) and opened in 1882 to provide access to the area of Kingsland where large residences were being built. It is known locally as the 'penny bridge', although the toll has recently risen to 20p. In July 1918 Captain Collet, an old Shrewsbury School pupil, flew his aeroplane under the bridge a number of times to celebrate successes in the Great War.

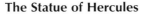

The Statue of Hercules
This copy of the marble Farnese Hercules statue in Museo Nazionale in Naples was cast in lead in Rome around 1650. It stood in front of Condover Hall until 1804, when it was sold to a local plumber as scrap metal. It was rescued by the Governor of Shrewsbury Prison and stood outside the prison for a while before being purchased by the Mayor and sited at the entrance to the park opposite St Chad's. It was moved to its present location in 1881.

Clement Memorial
This monument was built by public subscription to celebrate the life of William James Clement FRCS, a surgeon in the town who was educated at Shrewsbury School. He was Mayor of Shrewsbury 1862-63 and presented the chain of office still worn today by the Mayor. He went on to become a most popular Member of Parliament for the Borough 1865-70.

Greyfriars Footbridge

Greyfriars Bridge was opened on 1 January 1880 and replaced the ferry which crossed at this point to give access to the town for residents of Coleham and Belle Vue. It is a hog-backed pratt truss (lattice girder) bridge on solid masonry piers and has a span of 150 feet. There is a wonderful display of weeping willow trees on the far bank along this stretch of the river.

Greyfriars Friary

The Greyfriars (Franciscans) built a friary on the river in 1245 with a private gate in the town walls to give them access to the town. The role of the Order was to give service to the community through their vows of poverty, chastity and obedience. A local dignitary, Sir John de Charlton, was an early patron of the Order, and presented the friary with the magnificent Jesse window which is now in St Mary's church. The establishment was dissolved in 1538 along with two other friaries in the town as part of Henry VIII's Dissolution of the Monasteries.

The English Bridge from the South

This seven-arched stone bridge is the third one to be built at this point – the first being built on the site of a ford by monks building the abbey. The Stone Bridge, as it was called, was replaced by a second bridge in 1768-74 using local Grinshill stone. In the early part of the twentieth century this bridge was found to be too steep and narrow for the increased traffic on this major route between London and Holyhead. It was therefore dismantled and the current bridge erected, reusing the facing and much of the stone of the old bridge.

The English Bridge from the North
The new English Bridge was opened on 16 September 1927 at a cost of £80,000. The formal opening by the
Prince of Wales had been planned for October 1927, but was cancelled because of the death of his uncle, the
Marquis of Cambridge, who lived locally. However, since Queen Mary had crossed the bridge on 13 August 1927 while
under the final stages of its construction, it was decided to erect a plaque to say she had "opened" the bridge on that date.

St Mary's Water Gate (Traitor's Gate)

This gate in the town walls led down to the river. It was here that a traitor inside the town opened the gates to allow foot soldiers of the Parliamentarian Army to enter the town and capture it from the Royalist forces. The traitor is thought to have been Tom Turner, son of a barrister of the same name who was a staunch Royalist. Tom died at Lilleshall a month later fighting with the Parliamentarian Army. The attack on the town took place early in the morning of 22 March 1645. Resistance was slight and there were few casualties on either side.

Railway Bridges
The central stone bridge was built to carry the Shrewsbury to Birmingham Railway in 1849. Two additional iron bridges were erected on either side of the stone bridge to carry new platforms when the railway station was enlarged in 1899-1900. Shrewsbury is believed to be the only station in the country which has platforms extending over a river.

Castle Walk Footbridge
The present structure was built in 1951 to replace a traditional steel bridge giving access to the town from Underdale. It is a 250 foot long concrete bridge consisting of two pre-stressed cantilevers supporting a post-tensioned midspan section. At the time of its building this was an advanced design and may have been the first of its type in the country. It was designed by the well-known London firm of civil engineers Mott, Hay and Anderson.

Shrewsbury Castle

MEDIEVAL SHREWSBURY

Soon after the Norman Conquest, William the Conqueror gave Shrewsbury and most of Shropshire to his kinsman, Roger de Montgomery, and created him Earl of Shrewsbury. The town was then under constant siege by English and Welsh rebels, and one of Roger's first acts was to build a massive timber motte and bailey castle to command the two fords over the river – razing 50 houses to the ground to do so. The first stone castle on the site was built by Henry II in 1150-89, and extended by Edward I about 1300. Shrewsbury prospered throughout the early middle ages with the rise in population and increased demand for market products. All five of the original Saxon churches within the town were rebuilt during this period.

The castle ramparts dominate the only land entrance into the town. They are an imposing sight with two drum towers flanking the outer wall of the Great Hall.

Entrance to the Inner Bailey

Shrewsbury Castle formerly had an inner and an outer bailey. The inner bailey remains intact, but the outer bailey has been built over – although its original lines can be easily determined. The curtain wall in the picture separated the inner and outer baileys, and the lofty Norman gateway is now the main entrance to the castle. The heavy door to this gateway, which was rebuilt by Charles I at the start of the Civil War, was indented by musket balls probably during the attack on the castle in 1645.

The Great Hall and Inner Bailey

The Great Hall was originally built by Edward I in the early thirteenth century. It fell into decline after the conquest of the Welsh, and wasn't restored until 1565 when the castle was leased by Elizabeth I to a wealthy local merchant, Richard Onslow, who added the third storey. It was converted into a private residence by Thomas Telford for Sir William Pulteney MP, reputedly the wealthiest commoner in England, in the late eighteenth century. It is now the Regimental Museum of the Shropshire Regiments and houses a fine collection of militaria.

Laura's Tower

Laura's Tower was built on the site of the original Norman motte (keep) by Thomas Telford as a birthday present for Laura, daughter of Sir William Pulteney, as a place where she could paint and do her needlework. It is open to the public in September each year during Shrewsbury's Heritage Days. There are wonderful panoramic views from the tower across Shropshire and into the Welsh hills.

The Town Walls

The town walls were built in the early part of the thirteenth century for defence against the Welsh insurgents. These well preserved parts of the wall run alongside a road of the same name which follows the line of the original town wall. Much of the wall has been destroyed or built over, but good examples can still be found around the town. Probably the most unique use of these defences is by the burger chain McDonalds' in Pride Hill where you can sit in part of the foundations.

Thirteenth Century Watch Tower

This last surviving watch tower on Shrewsbury's medieval town walls was probably added during the reign of Henry III (1207-72). When the towers ceased to have a defensive role they were rented to principal townsmen by the Corporation. This tower was converted into a private dwelling by John Humphreys of Swan Hill Court and provided accommodation for his coachman. The arrow slits on the south side were made into windows at this time. The tower was left to the National Trust in 1930 by his daughter, Rachel Humphreys, and is open to the public six days a year. It is well worth visiting.

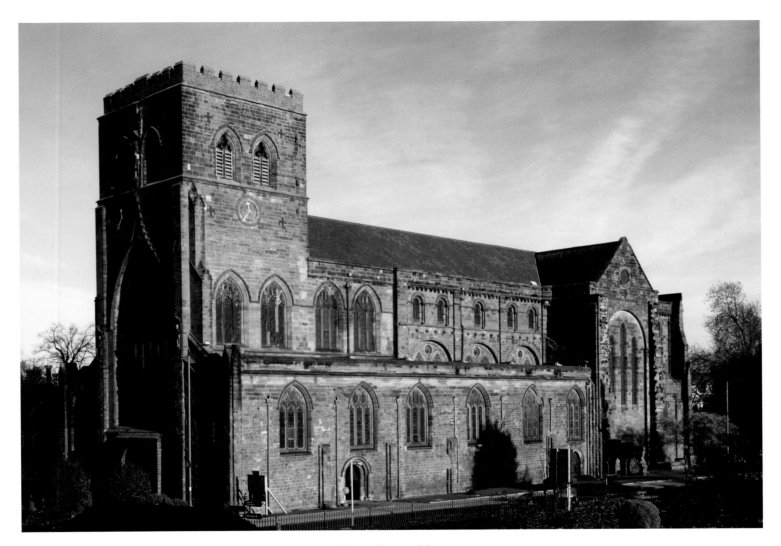

Shrewsbury Abbey

The Benedictine Abbey of St Peter and St Paul is the oldest building still standing in the town. It was founded by Roger de Montgomery in 1083, and stands outside the loop of the river near the English Bridge on the site of a wooden Saxon Church. Roger took his vows as a monk three days before his death in 1094, and was buried in the nave. Edward I summoned an historic Parliament at the abbey in 1283, which for the very first time included Commoners, for the purpose of trying the Welsh prince, David Llewelyn. The prince was subsequently executed at the top of Pride Hill.

The Nave

Since local people had been allowed to worship in the abbey from a very early date, the nave was left to serve as a parish church when the monastery was dissolved in 1540. This view from the west door shows the original Norman arches looking towards the east end, which was reconstructed by the Victorian architect, J. L. Pearson, in 1886-7. In recent years the abbey has become famous as the home of the fictional character, Brother Cadfael, attracting visitors from all over the world.

The Refectory Pulpit

The remains of the early fourteenth century refectory pulpit, which survived the dissolution of the abbey and the later road construction by Thomas Telford, lie in the car park across the road from the abbey. It is believed to be one of only three refectory pulpits still in existence, and the best preserved of them. Its distance from the main building gives one some idea of the massive scale of the abbey complex in its heyday.

St Mary's Church

The current St Mary's church began as a cruciform church about 1150 and was built on the site of a stone Saxon church dating from about 970. The red sandstone part of the tower dates from 1170 and contains masonry from Wroxeter Roman city. The whiter stonework above, including the spire, is fifteenth century. The spire is the third tallest in England, and it was from this spire that a steeplejack called Robert Cadman fell to his death in 1739 whilst entertaining the locals. This beautiful church is still consecrated but is now cared for by the Churches Conservation Trust.

The Nave

As you enter the church of St Mary's through the west door the nave stretches before you with its graceful arches ahead and alongside, with a fine view of the Jesse window in the distance. The floor tiles were made by Minton to a design by Maws of Jackfield. A beautiful carved oak ceiling with a profusion of birds, animals and angels soars above the nave. The roof was completely destroyed, and painstakingly rebuilt, after the top of the spire collapsed in a gale in 1896.

The Jesse Window

The magnificent fourteenth century Jesse east window, which portrays the genealogy of Christ, is the most important treasure of St Mary's church. A vine issues from the reclining figure of Jesse to form a series of oval spaces within the four central columns with each space containing the figure of a king. The two outer columns on each side contain figures of prophets. The family of Sir John Charlton of Powys, who commissioned the window for the Greyfriars chapel, are depicted along the bottom of the window. The window was moved to Old St Chad's church after the dissolution of the friary in 1538, and moved again to St Mary's in 1792 after the collapse of St Chad's.

Jesse
The reclining figure of Jesse. 'Isaiah 11.1 – and there shall come forth a rod out of the stem of Jesse and a branch shall grow out of his roots.'

St Bernard Window, South Nave Aisle *(right)*
St Mary's church is exceptionally rich in stained glass, and has the finest collection of continental glass in the country. The most interesting and valuable of this are the sixteenth century windows with scenes from the life of St Bernard of Clairvaux which were originally in the abbey church of Altenberg, near Cologne. The top of the centre light of this window depicts the scene at the abbey of Foigny where St Bernard 'excommunicated flies filling the building'. A man can be seen shovelling out the dead flies. This window was taken down and exhibited in Paris in 1990 for the 800th anniversary of St Bernard's death, and again in Cologne in 2007 for a Renaissance exhibition.

Saxon Grave Slab
Two Saxon grave slabs were unearthed during restoration work in the nineteenth century. This one depicts two snakes each devouring the other's tail and a type of knot with no beginning or end, representing eternal life.

The Font *(left)*
This beautiful fifteenth century octagonal font has an open arcading stem with ornate floral carving on the bowl.

St Alkmund's Church

The first church on this site was founded by Aethelfleda, daughter of King Alfred, in 912, and was dedicated to St Alkmund, a Northumbrian prince who was murdered near Derby c800. This was replaced by a fine Norman church, of which only the tower and spire remain. Scared by the almost total collapse of Old St Chad's in 1788, the church authorities decided to demolish the body of the church and rebuild it in Gothic revival style in 1793-5. The rebuild was probably unnecessary and cost twice as much as the original estimate.

**The East Window of
St Alkmund's Church**
This beautiful painted window by
Francis Eginton was installed in 1795
and represents an emblematic figure of
Faith. It was copied from the Madonna
in Guido Reni's 'Assumption' in Munich.
Four of the original cast-iron window
frames, which were made at
Coalbrookdale in 1795, still survive –
two at the east end and one either side
of the main door.

St Julian's Church

This church is adjacent to St Alkmund's and was dedicated to St Juliana, a fourth century virgin martyr of Nicodemia. The red sandstone base of the Norman tower dates from about 1200, and the yellow sandstone upper part from the fifteenth century. It was originally intended to have a spire. The main body of the church was rebuilt to a classical design by Thomas Farnolls Pritchard in 1749-59, with additional brick and stone facings added in 1846. The church is no longer in daily use.

Old St Chad's Church
The Lady Chapel is all that is left above ground of the massive medieval church of St Chad's, built in the early thirteenth century. The tower of this church collapsed as the clock struck at 4.00 am on 9 July 1788, causing such devastation that the nave had to be demolished. The famous engineer, Thomas Telford, had advised the church authorities a few weeks earlier that the tower was unsafe and should be taken down and re-built, but they unwisely chose to ignore his advice.

The Abbot's House

This is one of Shrewsbury's finest buildings, built in 1458-9 on land owned by Lilleshall Abbey. A fine example of a building jettied at two levels, it consists of a ground floor of shops with chambers above, and a third storey which may have been the abbot's town residence – well away from the noise and smells of the street. The fifteenth century shop fronts, with their divided doors and wide oak sills for displaying goods, are a wonderful example of butchers' shops of the period. Some of the original meat hooks still survive above the windows.

Fish Street

The land on which this street was built was also owned by Lilleshall Abbey, and the Three Fishes pub sign was once the abbey's emblem. The shops and houses date from the fifteenth century and include double-piled and jettied buildings. Stucco covers some of the original timber-framing but the character and original atmosphere of a medieval street is retained.

Henry Tudor House
This house on Wyle Cop dates from 1430-1 and is reputedly where Henry Tudor stayed on his way to the Battle of Bosworth in 1485. It is jettied at both first and second floor levels and has a wide cart entrance leading into Barracks Passage where the commercial buildings stood. The great hall was on the first floor level above shops, and the principal room was obviously lit by the fine medieval traceried windows.

Mytton's Mansion

This fine range of early fifteenth century timber-framed buildings lies below Henry Tudor House. It was once the home of Thomas Mytton, Bailiff of Shrewsbury in 1485 when Henry Tudor demanded entry into the town. Mytton, who boasted that Henry would only enter the town over his dead body, is said to have lain down on the old English Bridge and allowed Henry to walk over him.

Bear Steps Hall
This complex at the junctions of Butcher Row, Fish Street and St Alkmund's Square, known as the Bear Steps, has a range of building dates including the earliest scientifically-dated timber building in the town of 1358-9. Other parts of the complex are fourteenth century through to 1601. The whole complex was saved from demolition in 1968 by the Shrewsbury Civic Society, who carried out its restoration. It now houses their offices and a gallery.

Bear Steps

The Bear Steps connect St Alkmund's Square with Fish Street and are a prominent landmark in Shrewsbury. They are named after the Bear Inn which once stood at the bottom of the steps.

The Nags Head

The Nag's Head Inn and Hall are thought to have been part of the same building programme. The part now forming the Nags Head Inn has a deep front jetty, and restoration work revealed some fine cusped bracing. The timber frames were covered with new stucco after the restoration work was completed. The upper room is reputedly haunted, and three people are said to have committed suicide while staying there. The remains of the hall house dated 1419 stand at the rear of the inn.

King's Head Inn, Mardol *(left)*

This double pile house dates from 1404, the year following the Battle of Shrewsbury, and is one of the oldest inns in Shrewsbury. The double jettying shows up well in this image. The inn sign depicts Henry VII in recognition of his entry into the town up The Mardol in 1485 on his way to the Battle of Bosworth. This inn is also said to be haunted, although by a benign spirit.

King's Head Inn – Mural

This fine mural depicting the Last Supper dates from 1450-1520 and was found during restoration work in the 1970s. It may well have been moved and hidden here at the time of the Dissolution of the Monasteries to save it from wanton destruction.

Grope Lane at Night
Many ancient towns had Grope Lanes which were the haunt of prostitutes. Most towns changed the name to Grape or Green Lane, but thankfully Shrewsbury has retained the original name.

Barracks Passage
This runs under Henry Tudor House and its name is thought to commemorate the billeting of the future Henry VII's troops there in 1485 on their way to the Battle of Bosworth.

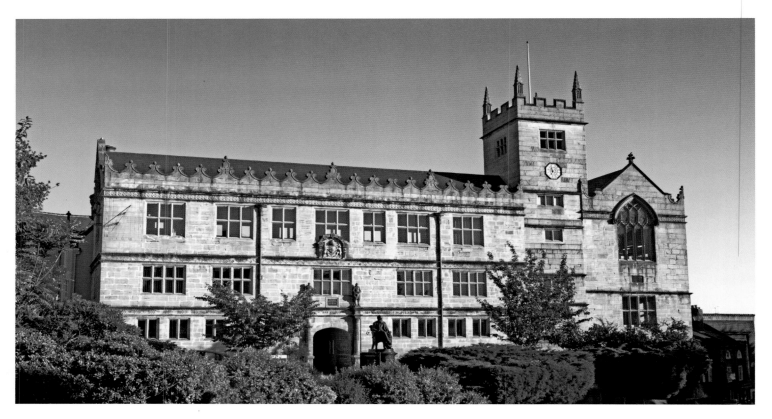

Old Shrewsbury School

THE TUDOR AND JACOBEAN TOWN

The renowned architectural historian Sir Nicklaus Pevsner, writing in 1935, accepted Shrewsbury's claim to be 'England's finest Tudor town' and thought it 'exceedingly fine'. Although some of the fine houses that he saw were destroyed in the 1960s, many beautiful timber-framed buildings remain, such as Ireland's Mansion, Rowley's House and the Drapers' Hall. They are much better preserved now than they were in Pevsner's time.

Shrewsbury Grammar School was founded by Edward VI in 1552 following the Dissolution of the Monasteries. Its royal patronage attracted large numbers of students and by 1586 it had become 'the largest school in all England'. It was initially established in existing buildings in the town and extended between 1595 and 1630 with these buildings on Castle Street. The school remained here until 1882 when it moved to its present location in Kingsland. The buildings were restored in the 1980s and are now the Public Library.

Philomathes and Polymathes

These two statues represent a student with his hat face down entering the school and the scholar with his hat face up leaving the school. Between them is a plaque with the date 1630 and a Greek inscription of Isocrates, an Athenian orator, which translates 'If you are eager to learn, you will learn much.'

Rigg's Hall *(right)*

Rigg's Hall was one of three buildings used by Shrewsbury School when it first opened. It is built on the old town wall, and parts of it date from 1405. The building was completely restored in the 1980s and linked to the stone school building. It is now used as a children's library.

The Old Market Hall

A new stone market hall was erected in The Square in 1596 as a joint venture between the Town Corporation and the Drapers' Guild, replacing a timber building dating from the 1260s on the same site. It is built of Grinshill stone and has an open ground floor which was used for the corn market, and an upper room, supported on Tuscan columns, which was used for wool sales. It was used as a Magistrates Court from 1870 to 1995 after the wool trade had declined. It was sympathetically restored and converted into a delightful cinema and café in 2004. This has proved extremely popular and is a valuable asset to the town.

Duke of York's Statue
This statue is thought to be of either the Duke of York (father of Edward IV and Richard III) or of the Black Prince, and was formerly on the old St George's Bridge. It was moved here in 1791. The coats of arms below it are those of England and Shrewsbury.

Coat of Arms
The coat of arms on the side of the hall is that of Queen Elizabeth I, surmounted by two Tudor roses.

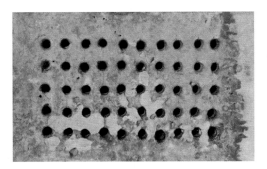

Counting Frame
This counting frame is built into the inner wall on the ground floor and was used with pegs for counting sacks of corn.

The Old House

The Old House on Dogpole is an L-shaped timber-framed house of the early sixteenth century with a cobbled inner courtyard and a river range of the early seventeenth century. The chimneys have tall triple-clustered star-shaped shafts, and there is a fine fireplace inside dated 1553. Mary Tudor stayed here when visiting Shrewsbury as a princess in 1526 at a time when it belonged to the Rocke family, servants to Catherine of Aragon.

The Gatehouse to the Council House
This fine building on Castle Street dates from 1610 and has heavy carving, Jacobean in style, depicting mermaids, griffins and grotesque figures. The gable is carved with a vine design and the finials are an armed knight and a key, denoting that it was once a prison.

The Old Council House
The Council House was built in 1502 within the outer bailey of the castle to provide a base for the Council of the Marches (established by Edward IV) when it sat in Shrewsbury. Two English kings, Charles I and James II, stayed here during visits to the town. The main frontage is onto the river, high above St Mary's Water Lane. The house was once the official residence of the Roman Catholic Bishop of Shrewsbury and is now private residences.

Perche's Mansion
The long mansion at the top of St Mary's Watergate was originally part of a U-shaped complex around a courtyard. It dates from 1581 and was built by John Perche, a bailiff of the town on four occasions. It was from this house that Tom Turner is thought to have let in the Parliamentary Army on 16 March 1645 through what is now called Traitor's Gate.

Greyhound Chambers
This building in Butchers' Row is an excellent sixteenth century example of the unifying effect of a long continuous jetty on an irregular building. The first floor overhang is unusually broad. Five rectangular bay windows on the first storey help to support the second, which also has a big overhang.

Castle Gates House
This early seventeenth century house originally stood in Dogpole. It was taken down and re-erected in Castle Street by the third Earl of Bradford in 1702, reputedly for his mistress, Ann Smith. The bay windows were added in 1912. It has a fine internal staircase.

The Drapers' Hall

The Drapers' guildhall in St Mary's Place, thought to be second on the site, was erected by the Guild in the late sixteenth century. The Drapers, who received their charter in 1462, had gained a near monopoly of the border cloth trade by this time and emerged as the most powerful members of Shrewsbury society. The Guild undertook much charitable work, and they still manage and support almshouses in the town. This is the last remaining guildhall in Shrewsbury and is still used by the Guild for their meetings.

Drapers' Hall – the Hall

The main hall contains some of original furniture created for the Guild. It includes a 17 foot long table with matching bench made in 1635, a 9 foot dais table made in 1662 together with a master's chair of the same date, and an unusual chest made in 1637 to hold the Guild's deeds and records. The hall has a simple and attractive stone fireplace dating from 1658.

Cromwell's Hotel

This hotel on Dogpole is an early seventeenth century two-storeyed, timber-framed house with three gables which has been covered with stucco. As timber-framed buildings ceased to be fashionable in Georgian times many were encased in a brick façade. If this proved too expensive, the outside façade would be plastered over.

Prince Rupert Hotel

The original mansion on St Mary's Street was built at the beginning of the seventeenth century by Edward Jones, a wealthy draper and brother of Thomas Jones who was appointed the first mayor of Shrewsbury by Charles I in 1639. The front of the mansion has been obscured by later alterations and the rest of the building has been heavily restored. Prince Rupert of the Rhine, nephew of King Charles I, lived here during the Civil War while in command of Royalist troops. His army looted the town and countryside and were very unpopular.

Cellars under Prince Rupert Hotel

The extensive range of cellars dates back to earlier buildings of the thirteenth century. They were excavated in 1971 while the building was being restored and were found to contain a number of fine pots dating from the tenth to the sixteenth centuries. The cellars are said to be heavily haunted.

Ireland's Mansion

This is perhaps the grandest of all Shrewsbury's timber-framed buildings. It was built in the High Street by Robert Ireland, a Shrewsbury wool merchant, in 1575 and was probably a speculative build as it has a large central house with two flanking tenements. A lot of timber uprights were used on the front of the house to show off the owner's wealth. There are some fine examples of medieval carpenters' marks inside one of the doorways.

67

Owen's Mansion

The three storeyed and jettied 1592 building on the left of the image, across the road from Ireland's Mansion, is a fine example of local carpentry with star patterning, quatrefoils, cable moulding and close studding. The 1598 extension on the right has a distinct change of style with the introduction of a row of squat baluster work. The gables are beautifully carved with a vine pattern and there are fine finials, probably of family members, on each of them.

Former Cross Keys Inn
This 1575 building stands at the bottom of Grope Lane opposite The Square. When it was restored in 1990 the beams were carved with modern political and environmental designs. The roundel of Margaret Thatcher and Michael Heseltine is a humorous record of the restoration date.

The Old Plough Inn
The two lower floors of this inn on The
Square date from 1575 and have all the
fine carpentry details seen on buildings
of that date. The third storey was added
in 1898 and was extremely well done.
The inn was only closed in 2004.

Rowley's House

This magnificent mansion on Shoplatch was built about 1590 by Roger Rowley, a rich draper, brewer and maltster. It is timber framed, almost exclusively with vertical members, and may have been built earlier. It was saved from demolition in 1932 and underwent a major restoration. It is currently the town's Museum and Visitor Information Centre.

Rowley's Mansion

Rowley's Mansion was built by Roger's son in 1618 and was reputedly the first brick mansion in the town. It was much restored in the 1930s using timbers from demolished buildings.

St Chad's Church from Kingsland

GEORGIAN SHREWSBURY

Daniel Defoe, the author of Robinson Crusoe, wrote after visiting Shrewsbury in 1725: 'This is a rich town full of gentry and yet full of trade too. It is a town of mirth and gallantry.' After a century of mayhem, society was travelling more and recognised the qualities that Shrewsbury had to offer. Many of the gentry built fine town houses to occupy during the season. Gardens became popular and walks were created for promenading. The Town Corporation had plenty of money to spend on municipal improvements. They installed new water supplies and oil lamps in the streets, and introduced rubbish collection. Trade boomed to meet the needs of a growing affluent society.

St Chad's church is the only Grade I Listed circular church in the country, and is surely one of the most beautiful Georgian churches in England. This image was taken from the roof of Shrewsbury School.

St Chad's Church from the Quarry

After the collapse of Old St Chad's in July 1788, the church committee decided to build a new church on a different site and invited the Scottish architect George Steuart to submit designs. Steuart submitted four designs, one conventional design and three designs with circular naves. The committee almost unanimously selected the conventional design, but by some sleight of hand Steuart tricked them into accepting a circular one. The church is built of brick and faced with Grinshill stone. The foundation stone was laid on St Chad's Day, 2 March 1790, and the church was consecrated on 19 August 1792.

St Chad's, the Vestibule

St Chad's is entered through a stately portico with four Doric columns carrying a heavy pediment. The square tower is surmounted by a cupola and rises 150 feet high. It is joined to the 100 feet diameter circular nave by an elliptical vestibule. Today the vestibule acts as a reception area and bookstall, and incorporates two arms of a fine staircase sweeping up to the gallery with rails of elegant Shropshire ironwork. Members of local regiments who fell in two world wars are commemorated on the wall and in memorial books.

The Chancel, St Chad's

The chancel is set back from the nave under an archway flanked by tall Corinthian pillars and pilasters. The superb sanctuary window is the work of David Evans, a local nineteenth century stained and enamelled glass artist, and is a copy of Ruben's 'Descent from the Cross' in Antwerp Cathedral. The central window depicts five disciples removing the body of Christ from the cross with the women looking on. The reredos was carved as a war memorial in 1923 and was coloured and gilded in 1951.

St Chad's, the Gallery
The impressive nave has very considerable horizontal and vertical spaces. The gallery rests on short Ionic columns on which in turn stand slender Corinthian columns supporting the ceiling. The columns have an iron core sheathed in deal wood and were manufactured in the nearby town of Ironbridge. This was a very unusual form of construction at the time and gives the church a light, airy feeling. The flat ceiling has a plaster moulded border of acanthus and a gilded sunburst with cherubs in the centre.

Royal Salop Infirmary

Shrewsbury was the fifth town outside London to have its own infirmary, which was established in 1747 in a large house on this site. This was replaced by the current building, with its impressive Doric portico, in 1826-30. It was designed by Edward Haycock and was one of the first buildings in the country to have a hot water central heating system. It received its royal title from King George V during a visit in June 1914. The hospital closed its doors in 1977 and is now a boutique shopping centre with apartments above.

The Lion Hotel

The main part of the Lion was built by Thomas Farnolls Pritchard in 1771 on the site of an older inn. The proprietor, Robert Lawrence, was the driving force behind developing it as a centre for coach travel and when Earl Temple, the Lord Lieutenant of Ireland, chose to use the Lion it became the most fashionable overnight stop on the London to Holyhead route. Many famous people have stayed there, including Charles Dickens, Benjamin Disraeli, Charles Darwin and Jenny Lind. The Lion now incorporates a fifteenth century building (in the centre) and a private house also built by Thomas Farnolls Pritchard in 1752.

79

Newport House

In 1696, the Earl of Bradford decided to build a new town house in Dogpole, on the same site as the house which he had moved to Castle Gates (see p.62). His new home was built in fashionable brick and was perfectly up to date in the London sense. It is virtually square and has five bays on each side. The porch of cast iron was added in the early nineteenth century. The house was used for many years as the Borough Council offices and was known as the Guildhall. It reverted to private ownership in 2004.

No. 4 Belmont

This is a wonderful example of a timber-framed building, the front of which was clad in brick in the early eighteenth century to bring it up to date with other houses being built in the newly fashionable Belmont Street. The front depicts an eighteenth century, seven bay house with the middle three bays set closer together and surmounted by a pediment. It was used by the town's Liberal Club in recent years, and is now offices.

No. 6 Belmont

No. 6 Belmont was built in 1701 for the Scott family of Betton Strange as their town house. It is a three storey, six bay house with a parapet and is adorned with quoining and keystones. Like all houses in Belmont, the more impressive façade is on the river side. The house is known as the Judges' Lodgings because of its use over many years. It was used as the set for Scrooge's house in the 1984 film of Dicken's *Christmas Carol*.

Hardwick House

This grand house on St John's Hill was built in the early 1700s for the headmaster of Shrewsbury School. It is two storeys high with a further half storey above the main cornice, and is flanked by two handsome coach houses. The whole is more like a country house than a house in town. There is a beautiful eighteenth century raised summer house with a fireplace in the garden.

Murivance House

This was built by Edward Haycock in 1799 to comply with an endowment of £2,000 left by John Allatt, Gent, a former chamberlain of the borough, to provide a school 'for the clothing, instruction, and apprenticing of poor children'. The school had twenty boys and twenty girls who were taught separately in the central block. The headmaster and headmistress occupied the two wings. It remained as a school until 1930, and is now offices.

Swan Hill Court House

Swan Hill Court is the grandest eighteenth century house in Shrewsbury. It was built by Thomas Farnolls Pritchard for William Pulteney, Earl of Bath, in 1761 as his town house for political purposes. Termed 'rus in urbe' (a country house built in a town) it has two flanking wings pressed directly onto the main building with no connecting arcades. It is a fine example of Georgian symmetry. The main building is two and a half storeys high and is crowned by a huge pediment decorated with swags and a coat of arms. It is still privately owned.

The Crescent

Shrewsbury's attempt to emulate the great crescents of Bath. It is a very plain brick-built curving terrace of four houses built by Charles Bromfield in 1790 as a speculative venture. The main decorative features are the attractive Adam-inspired fanlights over the doors, which are matched by blind fanlights over the ground floor windows. Charles Darwin's elder sister, Marianne, was born here in 1798. It was used as Scrooge's nephew's house during the 1984 filming of *Christmas Carol*.

Crescent Place

This most sophisticated terrace, designed at the end of the Georgian period, faces The Crescent and has a sequence of porches, windows and blind arches on the stuccoed ground floor. The massive first floor windows are eye-catching and the whole terrace is impressive.

Bowdler's School

Bowdler's School, founded on Town Walls in 1724, was endowed in the will of Thomas Bowdler as a school 'for instructing, clothing, and apprenticing poor children of the parish of St Julian'. It has five bays with the two outer bays protruding and quoined, and a hipped roof, and is typical of the period. The dormer windows were added later.

Wolley's House

Wolley's House is an impressive three storey house in The Square dating from 1730 and is built of red brick with quoins and keystones over the windows. The parapet, hiding the roof, protrudes over the windows. The house was festooned with poultry and game for the 1984 film *Christmas Carol*, and is where Scrooge sends the boy to buy a fat goose for the Cratchetts.

College Hill House

This delightful small Georgian town house dates from the early eighteenth century, and is built of brick and faced with ashlar. It was formerly the home of Edward Hughes, a Councillor and Alderman of Shrewsbury for 33 years and Mayor in 1849-50. It was later used by the Shrewsbury Arts Society and as a Magistrates Court, before reverting to private ownership in 1991. It has since been beautifully restored.

Clive House

The original buildings on this site were part of the Old College of St Chad which was dissolved in 1547. They were converted into three houses in 1752, and the one facing the garden was given a Georgian façade. Lord Clive, who had recently returned from India, accepted an invitation to become Mayor of Shrewsbury in 1762, and rented the property as his town house. He served as Member of Parliament for the Borough on three occasions.

The Mount

Dr Robert Darwin built his family home here in 1797, and it became famous as the birthplace of his son, Charles, on 12 February 1809. It has been described as 'an uninspired three storey Georgian house of red brick, square, substantial and ugly.' However, the house enjoys great views while being hidden from the town side, and it had inspiring gardens where Charles developed his skills of observation and recording detail. It is to be hoped that the house and gardens will soon be restored and opened to the public.

No. 13 Claremont Hill
Charles Darwin attended school in this house in 1817 when it was the home of the Reverend Case, the Unitarian Minister. It was from here that he vividly recalled witnessing the funeral scene of a Hussar in St Chad's churchyard. The house was built for a draper in 1689 and is now privately owned.

Statue of Charles Darwin
This bronze statue sits outside the old Shrewsbury School (now the Town Library) which Darwin attended from 1818 to 1825. The sculptor was Horace Mountford, a local man, and the bronze was cast by Messrs Broad and Son of London. The hands are modelled on those of Darwin's son, Professor George Darwin, and the sides of the chair are embellished with ferns, corals, barnacles and orchids depicting some of Charles Darwin's studies. The statue was largely paid for by the Shropshire Horticultural Society, and was unveiled on 10 August 1897.

Shrewsbury Railway Station

VICTORIAN & MODERN SHREWSBURY

Shrewsbury ceased to be seen as a smart resort town in the nineteenth century as the social scene moved to the spa towns and seaside. Agriculture declined and new industries developed as a result of advances in technology. These included the Grade I listed Flax Mill at Ditherington – the world's first iron-framed building – and Hazeldine's celebrated iron foundry at Coleham. The arrival of the railway and the development of Shrewsbury as a major rail centre brought increased prosperity.

Shrewsbury Station was designed by Thomas Penson in a neo-Tudor style to match the former Shrewsbury School opposite, and was opened in 1849. The original design had only two storeys. The lower storey, which is now the ticket concourse, was added in 1901 by jacking up the original building and excavating underneath it – a very advanced procedure for the time.

Railway Station – Decorative Features

The station is built in Grinshill stone and is beautifully carved throughout. It is recognised as one of the architectural treasures of the railways and great care was taken to preserve its decorative features when the station was restored in the mid 1980s. The original platforms are adorned with carved heads of royalty.

Severn Bridge Junction Signal Box
This listed three storey signal box was built when the station was enlarged in 1901, and with 180 levers, it became the largest manual signal box in Britain. It is now believed to be the largest manual lever-operated signal box still in operation in the world. It has an unparalleled safety record and is expected to stay in use at least until the 2030s.

Roman Catholic Cathedral

The first Bishop of Shrewsbury was appointed by Pope Pius IX in 1850, and the Earl of Shrewsbury offered to build him a cathedral. The Earl chose the famous Victorian architect, Augustus Welby Pugin to design it, but both the Earl and Augustus died before work could begin. Pugin's son Edward took over his father's design, and the foundation stone was laid in December 1853. The cathedral was originally to have a 300 foot tower and spire, but the builders dug down 70 feet before giving up and the spire was abandoned.

Stained Glass

The cathedral has a wonderful collection of stained glass, including seven windows by the world renowned Arts and Crafts artist, Margaret Rope. The images shown are the west window, depicting saints and martyrs, and the South Aisle window. Margaret made stained glass windows for many churches and cathedrals around the world, including some in Canada, Australia and South Africa. She spent the last 30 years of her life as a Carmelite nun.

United Reformed Church
This church was consecrated as a Congregational
chapel in May 1864, and was joined with the
United Reformed Church in 1972. It is built in grey
Grinshill stone with bands of red sandstone, and is
the only non-conformist church in the town to have
a tower and spire. It dominates the view across
English Bridge towards the abbey.

St Nicholas Presbyterian Church

Pevsner calls this church 'atrocious neo-Norman, very tall, and so short from the side that it looks like a fragment'. A congregation of Presbyterians was established in the town in 1865 and they opened this church on Castle Street five years later. It is built on the site of the Norman chapel of St Nicholas in the outer bailey of the castle. It is now in commercial use.

101

Shrewsbury School Chapel

The chapel was built shortly after the school moved to its present site at Kingsland in 1882. It was designed by Sir Arthur Blomfield in red and yellow stone in grand gothic style with groups of narrow lancet windows. Many of the interior fittings were brought here from the old school chapel in the centre of the town. The school has a fine reputation for music and the chapel is one of three venues in the school where concerts are open to members of the public.

Hospital of the Holy Cross

These almshouse buildings opposite Shrewsbury Abbey were built in 1853, although the hospital was founded much earlier.
They are built of squared red sandstone with plain tiled roofs and beautifully carved chimneys. Their original purpose was
'for the residence of poor women aged 55 years and over who profess the Christian faith in accordance with the principles
of one of the Protestant denominations'. They are still in use.

Former Eye, Ear and Throat Hospital
This wonderful Victorian edifice was built on Town Walls by C. O. Ellison of Liverpool in 1879-81 and extended in 1926. It is built in the Gothic style in fiery red Ruabon brick with terracotta dressings, and has a polygonal tower on the corner of Kingsland Bridge Road. The building was converted to apartments when the hospital closed in 1999, and the tower, which had earlier collapsed, was rebuilt.

Coleham Pumping Station

Coleham Pumping Station, housing two massive steam driven beam engines, was built in 1900 to pump Shrewsbury's sewage under the river to a sewage works at Monkmoor. The engines consumed a ton of coal every day and required a team of seven men to keep them running. The pumps have been driven by electricity since the 1970s and are still in use today. The Pumping Station is now a Shrewsbury museum and the beam engines are fired up several times a year on public open days.

The Music Hall
The Music Hall was designed by Edward Haycock in the grand style and opened in November 1840. It incorporates parts of several other buildings, notably Vaughan's Mansion dating from the early fourteenth century. From the beginning it was known as 'That Fine Hall' and attracted national artists and performers. Charles Dickens gave a reading of his *Christmas Carol* here in 1858. The Music Hall was closed in 2009 when Theatre Severn opened, and it is currently being redeveloped into an exciting new Museum and Art Gallery which is due to open in late 2013.

Halifax Building Society
The Salop Fire Office (established in 1780)
and the Shropshire and North Wales
Assurance Company were united with the
Alliance Assurance Company in 1890. Their
new head office in the High Street was
designed by A. E. Lloyd Oswell in a Flemish
style and opened in 1891. The façade is
ornately carved and commemorates the
three former companies.

The Market Hall
The magnificent Corn Exchange and Market of 1869 – as impressive from the outside as a Gothic cathedral – was demolished in 1965 to make way for this ugly concrete building. However, the new market has attracted an excellent range of stalls and is doing well commercially at a time when most markets are in decline. It won an award in 2012 for the best publicly owned indoor market in the Midlands.

Lloyds Bank

Lloyds Bank was built at the bottom of Pride Hill in 1967 to replace a mock timber-framed building on the site – a development which caused much controversy in the town at the time. Surprisingly, it won a Civic Trust award for its design which was thought to reflect the jettying out of the first and second storeys and the close studding of the timbers on the Tudor buildings nearby.

The Entrance to the Castle

SHREWSBURY, TOWN OF FLOWERS

Shrewsbury today is a thriving market town and retail centre for much of Shropshire and Mid Wales. It has also become well known internationally as a Town of Flowers. The initiative for this is thought to have come from L/Bdr Tanswell, who wrote to the *Shrewsbury Chronicle* in 1944 from the front line in Burma: 'I am all for making Shrewsbury a Flower Town as part of its attraction. The lead is there with our wonderful flower show. I would like to see flower beds in every possible place…' His wish certainly came true. Shrewsbury won the prestigious Britain in Bloom competition in 1986 and 2006, and has won a host of awards at regional level. In 2007 it went on to win Gold Medal at the Entente Floriale (Europe in Bloom) and the International Challenge of the Communities in Bloom, under the chairmanship of co-author Stan Sedman.

The Town Council maintain the gardens at Shrewsbury Castle to an extremely high standard throughout the year. This image shows a fine display of spring flowers.

The Inner Bailey
Summer flowers in the Inner Bailey. The Town Council grow more than 300,000 plants
annually in their nurseries for use in public gardens at the castle and The Dingle.

The Dingle in Spring
This beautiful garden is set in the Quarry Park and attracts thousands of visitors throughout the year. It was originally created in 1881 on the site of a pool used for watering cattle.

The Dingle in Summer
Part of the formal gardens in summer. Percy Thrower re-designed the gardens when he was
Parks Superintendent 1946-1974, and there is a fine bronze bust of him in the gardens.

113

The Dingle in Autumn
This is a lovely time in The Dingle, when the Acers turn a rich autumnal colour.

The Dingle in Winter
A winter scene with St Chad's church in the background. This image was taken at Christmas 2010
when the trees were covered with a thick layer of hoar frost.

Flowers in the Square

L/Bdr Tanswell wrote in his letter to the *Shrewsbury Chronicle*: 'Imagine how well The Square would look with a splendid show of flowers in spring and summer and evergreen shrubs in winter.' As the recognised centre of the town, The Square is always ablaze with colour. The Town Council provides a range of tubs and floral towers and retailers sponsor hanging baskets.

Traffic Roundabouts
The traffic islands and roundabouts
around the town are always full of colour.
They are sponsored by local businesses
and provide funds for other projects
by Shrewsbury in Bloom.

Floral Trees
The Town Council has provided floral trees in several locations around the town. This one is at one end of Frankwell Footbridge.

118

Flowers on the Bridges
Both main road bridges are adorned with baskets
and the railings alongside Victoria Quay are
decorated with floral mangers.

**The Royal Oak and
the Shrewsbury Hotel**
Many local inns support the floral
theme of the town and these are typical
of the standards achieved. The Royal
Oak has won its category in the
Town of Flowers competition
on several occasions.

Edgefield Green Community Gardens
This group of 56 sheltered dwellings has reached an outstanding level of horticulture and has been commended by judging panels from Europe and North America as well as the United Kingdom. They received the Royal Horticultural Society's Award for Floral Excellence in 2009 in recognition of the standard they have achieved.

No. 41 Worcester Road

The occupants of this house, Mr and Mrs Brooks, regularly take part in Shrewsbury in Bloom competitions and have won many local and national awards over the years. Their hanging baskets are particularly fine.

Valducci Brugmansias

Mr Luigi Valducci grows many unusual plants and vegetables on his three allotments, but he has a passion for Brugmansias (Angels Trumpets). He holds the National Collection of these and has the largest private collection in Europe. He is a RHS Gold Medallist and a regular exhibitor at the Shrewsbury Flower Show. He opens his gardens annually under the National Gardens Scheme.

Shrewsbury Flower Show – Plant Heritage Garden

The Shrewsbury Flower Show is one of the Premier Summer Shows in the country and attracts exhibitors from across the country and beyond. It was established in 1875 and is now the world's longest running horticultural show. This exhibit by Plant Heritage (National Council for the Conservation of Plants & Gardens) won the Best in Show trophy. It features a contemporary garden with geometrical hard landscaping and contains many rare and unusual plants.

Shrewsbury Flower Show – Pheasant Acre Plants
This stunning display of gladiolus by Pheasant Acre Plants of Bridgend contains large, medium and nanus flowered plants.
Pheasant Acre Plants exhibit at the show every year and won Best in Show with this exhibit.

Shrewsbury Flower Show – Phillip Tivey & Son
This is a small part of a stunning display of Alstroemerias by Phillip Tivey of Leicester, who exhibit at the show every year. It was awarded the Society's Large Gold Medal.

The Old Work, Wroxeter Roman City

ENVIRONS OF SHREWSBURY

Shrewsbury is an excellent base for visiting Shropshire's two outstanding tourist attractions: the World Heritage Site of Ironbridge Gorge, the 'Birthplace of Industry', 16 miles to the east, and the Shropshire Hills Area of Outstanding Natural Beauty 15 miles to the south. There are also a number of sites closer to the town that are well worth visiting. All the buildings mentioned below are listed Grade I by English Heritage.

Wroxeter Roman City (or Viriconium) was once the fourth largest town in Roman Britain. It began as a legionary fortress and developed into a thriving civilian city. Although much still remains below ground, the most impressive features today are the second century municipal baths and the remains of a huge wall, known as the Old Work, which is one of the largest freestanding pieces of masonry left in Britain.

The Main Baths Complex
The baths were constructed between 120 and 150AD to a standard plan used throughout the western part of the Roman Empire. The tiled pillars in the picture supported the floor of the main heated rooms where bathers gathered in the hot, humid atmosphere to sweat out the dirt – much like Turkish baths today.

The Roman Villa
The Roman villa was built in 2010 for a BBC2 series, using only techniques known to have been used throughout Roman Britain at the time. The house has an oak frame covered with painted lime plaster, one frame of which has been left exposed. A stone-built bath house lies at right angles to the main building. The floor plan was based on that of a town house excavated at Wroxeter in 1913-4.

Moreton Corbet Castle
The Keep (left)   **The Gatehouse** (right)

The ruins of Moreton Corbet Castle and its attached mansion form one of the most picturesque of Shropshire's castle sites. The castle was originally triangular in shape and was surrounded by a moat, traces of which can still be seen. The keep dates from c1200 and is two (formerly three) storeys high. Only its north face and fragments of the east and west walls survive. The castle and hall were destroyed by Parliamentary forces in 1644 and were never rebuilt.

Moreton Corbet Hall
This stately Italianate mansion was built by Sir Robert Corbet in the 1570s, and may have been designed by him. As a diplomat he had travelled widely and was said to have been "carried away with the affectionate delight of the architecture" he found in Italy. He died of the plague in 1583 without seeing his home completed. The Hall is still owned by the Corbet family, but is maintained by English Heritage.

131

Acton Burnell Castle – North Side

These are the remains of a fortified manor house built in the thirteenth century by Robert Burnell, Bishop of Bath and Wells, and Lord Chancellor of England 1274-92. He was a close friend and confidant of Edward I for more than thirty years. When the king was staying at Acton Burnell in the autumn of 1283, he summoned one of the first parliaments to be attended by Commoners. It passed a law for the protection of creditors which became known thereafter as the Statute of Acton Burnell.

Acton Burnell Castle – Interior
The castle was built of grey and red sandstone and was three storeys high with a tower at each corner. The ground floor housed a buttery and other domestic rooms, and the Great Hall was on the first floor with the bishop's private apartments above it. The castle was finally abandoned in 1672, and was used thereafter as farm buildings. It is also maintained by English Heritage.

Haughmond Abbey at Sunset

Haughmond Abbey began as a small religious community towards the end of the eleventh century, and was given abbey status in 1155. It became a prosperous community until dissolved in 1539 as part of Henry VIII's Dissolution of the Monasteries. Its new owner, Sir Edward Littleton, bought the abbey from the Crown and converted it to a private residence. It was burned down during the Civil War and was used thereafter as farm buildings. Sheep still graze in the cloisters.

The Abbot's House

The standing remains include the foundations and west doorway of the twelfth and fourteenth century church, the late twelfth century Chapter House, the early thirteenth century Refectory and the Abbot's Hall and House. The abbot's suite of rooms would have been decorated and furnished in an expensive manner appropriate to his status. The bay window was probably inserted in the late fifteenth century to replace a smaller, simpler version.

Haughmond Hill (above)
View from Haughmond Hill (left)
Haughmond Hill is a lovely wooded outcrop of very ancient Pre-Cambrian rock a few miles east of Shrewsbury. It is owned by the Forestry Commission, who have made it into a delightful forest park, with guided trails, car parking and a popular café. There is a small enclosure on the summit rock known as Queen Eleanor's Bower, from where the wife of King Henry IV is said to have watched the progress of the Battle of Shrewsbury. Although it is only 152 metres (500 feet) high, the views from Haughmond Hill across Shrewsbury to the Welsh hills are stupendous.

Attingham Hall at Dawn

Attingham Hall was built for the 1ˢᵗ Lord Berwick in 1785 by the Scottish architect George Stueart and was in continuous use by the family for more than 160 years until the title died out in 1953. The huge mansion was designed to impress, and its interiors reflect the Regency splendour of the time. The collections include ambassadorial silver, Italian furniture and Grand Tour paintings collected by the 3rd Lord Berwick. The National Trust Regional Headquarters is based at Attingham and they take very good care of the house and grounds.

Snowdrops in Attingham Park

The house looks out over 500 acres of parkland, artfully landscaped by the great Humphrey Repton. A copy of his famous Red Book is held there. The grounds include a walled vegetable garden, recently restored by the Trust, parkland and several acres of mixed woodland. There are some lovely walks through the woods and along the banks of the River Tern, ranging in length from one to three miles.

Attingham Deer Park
Attingham Deer Park lies across the River Teme from the house and is home to a herd of about 250 Fallow Deer. When Attingham was given to the Trust in 1947, one of the conditions was that they should keep the herd in perpetuity. This image shows three fine bucks, with The Wrekin in the background.

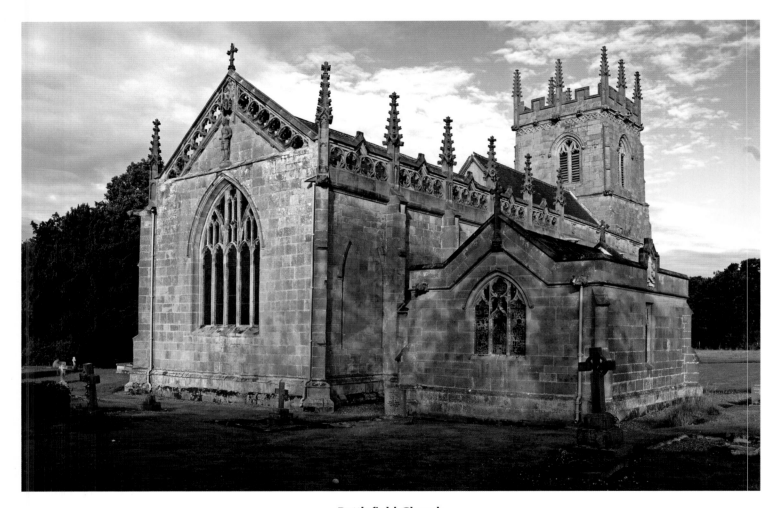

Battlefield Church

Three miles north of Shrewsbury you will find a church built in 1406 to commemorate the thousands of men who lost their lives on 21 July 1403 in the bloody Battle of Shrewsbury. The battle was fought between King Henry IV and a rebel army led by Harry Hotspur, and it was the first time the longbow had been used on English soil – with deadly results. There is an interpretive exhibition of the battle at Battlefield 1403 a few hundred yards north of the church, together with an excellent farm shop and restaurant.

Statue of King Henry IV
King Henry IV is commemorated with this statue
above the west window. There are shields of knights
who fought alongside him on the roof beams inside.

Fifteenth Century Pieta
The main treasure of the church is this beautiful
and moving oak pieta of the Virgin Mary mourning
the body of Christ after the crucifixion. It was
probably brought here from another church.

Langley Chapel

This chapel lies about one mile south of Acton Burnell Castle and dates from about 1370. It was re-roofed and refurnished by Sir Humphrey Lee of Langley Hall in 1601 and has been virtually unaltered since. The chapel fell into disuse after Langley Hall burned down during the eighteenth century, and it was finally abandoned in the nineteenth century. It fell into disrepair and in 1914 became one of the first buildings in the country to be rescued by being taken into the care of the Ministry of Works, a forerunner of English Heritage.

Langley Chapel – Interior

The chapel is unique in having a complete set of original seventeenth century wooden furnishings. These include a reader's desk, a large ornate box pew for the Lee family, smaller box pews for tenant farmers and wooden benches for labourers. Unusually, there is a raised musicians' pew at the rear. The altar was a simple communion table with benches around it as befits its Puritan heritage. The chapel is very atmospheric and well worth visiting.

Lyth Hill Countryside Park

Lyth Hill Countryside Park lies a couple of miles south of Shrewsbury and boasts some of the best panoramic views of the Shropshire Hills anywhere, from The Wrekin in the east, through Wenlock Edge and the Stretton Hills in the south, to the Stiperstones and Pontesbury Hill in the west. The park is owned by Shropshire Council and includes areas of woodland, scrub and open grassland. It is a very popular walking area for Shrewsbury people and is especially favoured by their dogs.